Needle Crafts 2

CANVAS WORK

SEARCH PRESS
Tunbridge Wells

INTRODUCTION

Canvas work is a centuries-old form of embroidery, usually in wool, on a specially-prepared fabric in which the stitches completely cover the canvas. Canvas work never remains quite the same; people constantly discover new stitches and things to make.

Some forms of canvas work are done in one stitch only: for example, petit point, gros point and Florentine (Bargello). It is also known as 'needlepoint' (which can be confused with needlepoint lace), or as 'tapestry' (which, strictly speaking, is woven).

Instructions are given for many canvas-work stitches, but these do not include dressmaking and other making-up techniques beyond the scope of this booklet.

MATERIALS

Canvas

Canvases are stiffened to make them easier to work. There are two main types: single (mono), or double (Penelope) in which the threads are woven in groups of two. Double canvases are useful for cross stitches but single canvases can be used for all stitches and are more generally useful. You can buy them in different widths, qualities and size of mesh and specialist embroidery shops offer the widest selection. If you can find off-cuts, buy a selection to try them out. Some cheap canvases are very stiff, wear out the yarn and are uncomfortable to use. If you are making something like a chair seat which will have to stand up to heavy wear, buy the best quality canvas.

Panel: 'Poppies'. Worked on 14s canvas in crewel wool, with some cotton perle *(by Nora Jones)*.

Canvas mesh sizes are quoted by numbers of holes (or threads) to 2.5 cm. Raffia canvas is coarse, with 10 holes to 2.5 cm. It is easy to see, quick to work and takes a variety of threads. When worked, it is fairly bulky and not suitable for small pieces or for more complicated shaped items. The finest canvas has 22 threads to 2.5 cm, takes longer to work and demands good sight but can be made up easily. Between the two extremes are single canvases with 12, 14, 16 and 18 threads to 2.5 cms.

Threads

Some wools are specially made for canvas embroidery. Crewel wool is a fine stranded wool and can be used with as few or as many strands in the needle as are needed to cover the canvas. It is versatile, hard-wearing and made in a wide range of colours, most of them soft and muted.

Tapestry wools are thicker and some brands include bright, clear colours. They give a smooth effect when worked but are not adaptable to all canvas mesh sizes.

Persian wool is a thicker stranded yarn which comes in three strands; the number in the needle can vary.

Two-ply rug wool can be used on the coarser canvases. It is hard-wearing. Off-cuts from carpet factories, called thrums, are cheaper than wool bought by the kilo. These are usually available in mixed colours only and the mixtures vary from time to time. Long thrums are the ones for canvas work; short thrums are only suitable for hooked rugs.

Most other threads can be used if they pass through the mesh of the canvas without distortion. If wear is a consideration, the choice must be restricted. Among embroidery and weaving threads some can be used to give sheen, *coton perlé* (pearl cotton) for example. The coarsest canvas takes synthetic raffia. Knitting and crochet threads give lots of possibilities and the oddments box in your wool shop will provide cheap yarns for experiments.

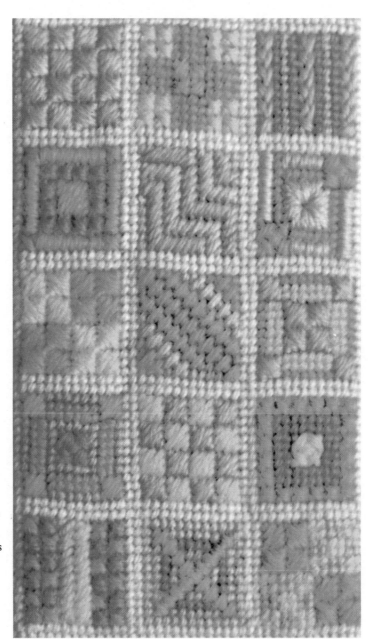

Box lid. Worked on 16s canvas in tapestry wools. The divisions were done first in two rows of tent stitch, leaving 12 threads for each square, which were filled to make a patch-work design. The edges of the canvas were laced over a piece of card, inserted in the recessed lid of the box, and glued in place
(by Diana Gill).

Sewing case. Worked on French single 18s canvas, originally a sampler of stitches and later made up, in worsted wool thrums and copper crochet thread *(by Jo Peterson)*.

Overleaf:
Pendant – gold/white. Worked on 22s canvas in stranded cotton and silk. The design was taken from a shell. Mounted on a brass jewellery mount over thin foam, backed with felt. A buttonhole loop is worked through the hole at the top to ensure the pendant hangs straight *(by Daphne Nicholson)*.

Pendant – green. Worked on 22s canvas in stranded cotton and coton perle. Design inspired by summer leaves. Mounted on a brass jewellery mount over thin foam, backed with felt. Finished with a handmade twisted cord, which is also used for the chain *(by Daphne Nicholson)*.

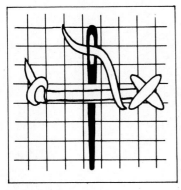

Fig. 1. Fastening on

Needles

A packet of assorted tapestry needles will give you the right size for most yarns. Especially large ones are made for primary-school use and these take two-ply rug wool. If you cannot get these, look for packets of assorted household needles. If you are joining canvas work to a fabric backing, chenille needles are needed. These look the same as tapestry needles with large eyes but have sharp points.

MAKING A START

Allow a good margin all round. For a small piece on the finest canvas, allow at least 2 cm. For a large piece, such as a chair seat, allow at least 5 cm all round. You may like to make one margin bigger to experiment with stitches to avoid unpicking on the work itself. Plan the work so that the selvedge runs downwards if possible. Canvas frays, so secure the edges at once by over-sewing by hand or by zigzag machining. Some people use adhesive tape.

Wool wears thin in passing in and out of the canvas, so avoid long lengths in the needle; 40 cm is about average. Some stitches, Florentine for example, are less hard on the wool and longer lengths can be used than, say, for tent stitch.

To thread the needle, double the wool round the eye and push the flattened double end through. Choose a needle that passes through the canvas easily. If it is too big, the wool will come out. If it is too fine, the wool will be hard to pull through the canvas.

Begin work by knotting the yarn and putting the needle through so that the first few stitches will cover the end on the back (*Fig. 1*). Then the knot can be cut off. Fasten off by darning the wool through the work on the back. You will need longer ends to begin and end if the stitch (Florentine, for example) is not very dense on the back.

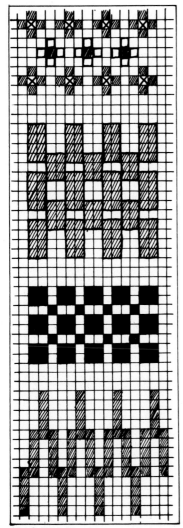

Fig. 2. Designing for cross stitch on graph paper

THE STITCHES

Some general advice

Don't try to learn too many stitches at once but see how many different effects you can get with each stitch. The canvas must be completely covered. This is done partly by choosing the right thickness of wool for the stitch and for the mesh of the canvas, and partly by the way the stitch is worked. The diagrams are drawn to show how the stitch is worked and so the wool does not always appear to cover completely. The needle is shown going into and out of the canvas in one movement. In practice, stitches usually look best if you put the needle through in one movement and bring it up in a second movement.

Remember that stitches are worked touching each other with no spaces or empty threads in between. If you want to try stitches before working something to use, get into the habit of working one block of stitches joined to the next.

Where possible, bring the needle up into an empty hole and down into a hole shared by a previous stitch. This makes a clear definition between the stitches. When the yarn twists up, allow it to hang free and untwist before going on.

Many stitches have more than one name; only one is given here in most instances.

If you begin by making something small, you will learn about stitches, yarns, design and making-up right from the beginning. This experience will help you progress towards bigger and more complicated work without making expensive mistakes.

Patterns in colour and texture

Patterns can be built up by using different colours or textures using one stitch only. You may like to work these out directly

Cushion with stitch patterns. A design based on areas of different stitches, divided by two rows of tent stitch *(by Mary Pick. Lent by the Schools Service Section, Reading Museum).*

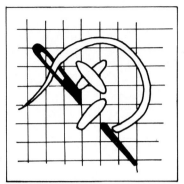

Fig. 3. Cross stitch

Fig. 4.(a). Crossed corners: *(b)* The order of crossing corners

Fig. 5. Double cross stitch

on the canvas or you may prefer to plan them on graph paper first (*Fig. 2*). If the size of the spaces on the paper is the same as the mesh of the canvas, the finished work will be the same size. If the mesh is smaller, you can calculate the finished size or work a trial area to see what the finished size will be. When working on graph paper, count each line as a thread of canvas.

Cross stitch (*Fig. 3*)

Work over two threads. The top thread always lies in the same direction all over the work and the stitch can be worked from right to left and from left to right in turn.

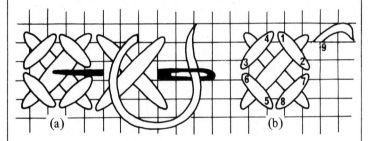

Crossed corners (*Fig. 4*)

A cross is worked over 4 threads and then the corners are crossed. Follow the same movements for each stitch to keep it even all over the work. Fig. 4a shows the order of crossing the corners. Try working this stitch in the same thread all over. Then try working the large crosses first (in a slightly thicker thread if you like), then work the corners in a different colour or tone of the same colour or a different texture.

Double cross stitch (*Fig. 5*)

This time a large cross over 4 threads is crossed by another large worked upright cross. A different thread may be used for the upright cross.

Hungarian stitch (*Fig. 6*)

This is worked in groups of 3 stitches separated by a hole. The second row of stitches is worked into the space so that all the small stitches are in the same vertical line and all the large stitches also lie underneath each other. This can be worked in the same colour all over or a second colour or a different texture can be used in alternate rows.

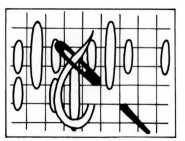

Fig. 6. Hungarian stitch

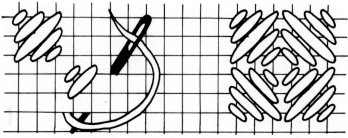

Flat stitch (*Fig. 7*)

This is worked on the diagonal over squares of three threads. The rows alternate. *Fig. 8* shows some of the possible variations on this stitch. Different colours or textures can be used for rows in each direction or half the stitch can be worked in one colour or texture and half in another. By using three or more different wools, you can create an illusion of depth. This can be emphasised by using a thicker wool for the longer stitches.

Fig. 7. Flat stitch

Fig. 8. Varying flat stitch. *(a)* Each row is worked in alternate dark and light wool; *(b)* one diagonal is worked in dark wool, the other in light; *(c)* the longest stitches are in a heavy wool. Each half of the pattern is worked in different but finer wools.

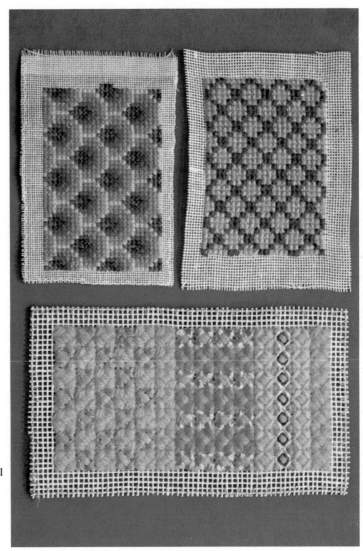

Samples *(top left)*. Cross stitch. 22s canvas. Crewel wool; *(Top right)* Cross stitch. 16s canvas. Crewel wool; *(below)* Crossed corners. 10s canvas. Knitting wool, dull and shiny synthetic raffia, tapestry wool, coton perle *(c)* Multiple cross, back, upright Gobelin, cross. 14s canvas. Crewel wools.

Florentine stitch (*Fig. 9*)

Florentine (Bargello) is a stitch that is worked in steps up and down the canvas. The diagram shows a simple form. Each stitch is made over 4 threads and the next stitch steps up or down 2 threads. The stitch is usually worked in several tones, shading from dark to light. These need not be all in the same range and the effect is livelier if the shades vary.

Patterns with combined stitches

Patterns can be built up by contrasting stitches. Some are raised, some smooth. Some of the stitches already introduced can be used together easily. In the patterns designed on graph paper, any of the blocks of 4 threads can be stitched in crossed corners with smaller blocks in cross stitch. Stripes can be made with flat stitch and double cross stitch.

Some of the smaller stitches give very different textures which are useful when combining stitches.

Tent stitch (*Fig. 10*)

This is also known as petit point. Single lines and tiny areas can be worked from left to right and right to left or top to bottom and *vice versa* (*Fig. 10a*). Notice that the stitch on the back is long and take care that when you change direction, you still make a long stitch on the back. This ensures an even texture and good covering power.

In large areas (*Fig. 10b*), the stitch is worked diagonally to avoid much of the distortion that tent stitch produces. Notice the angle of the needle in each row. This produces a woven look on the back.

Because it is so small, tent stitch is useful for making a flat texture against bulky stitches and for creating fine details.

Fig. 9. Florentine stitch

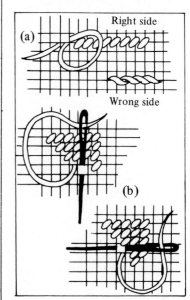

Fig. 10. Tent stitch. *(a)* Working from right to left. *Above:* the right side; *below:* the wrong side; *(b)* working diagonally for large areas

Case for a magnifying glass. Worked in various wools, gold kid, and silky threads on 16s canvas, lined with chamois leather *(by Lois Hennequin)*.

Church kneeler. One of a group made for the royal pew, the Chapel Royal, Hampton Court Palace (by permission). Worked on double canvas, 13 threads to the inch, using crewel wools and various canvas stitches. The design was based on the Tudor ceiling of the Chapel Royal, which is in a similar blue and gold *(by Rosemary Pedder)*.

Cushion with repeating pattern. Worked on 10s canvas in tapestry and 2-ply rug wool and coton perlé, using long-armed cross, slanted Gobelin, diamond eyelets, back, and crossed corners. The edging stitch joins the fabric back to the canvas work *(by Nora Jones)*.

Upright cross stitch (*Fig. 11*)

Another small stitch, this time with a knobbly effect. Each row is worked in the spaces created by the previous row. Notice that the second part of the stitch is worked as a back stitch.

Upright Gobelin (*Fig. 12*)

First take a thread over the area to be worked. Work each stitch over 2 threads, covering the long thread and producing a ribbed effect.

Encroaching Gobelin (*Fig. 13*)

A smoother effect is made by working a slanting stitch up 5 threads and across 1. The next row is worked into the previous one as in the diagram.

Bricking (*Fig. 14*)

Straight stitches worked over every other mesh with successive rows worked between give another different texture.

Knotted stitch (*Fig. 15*)

Worked over 3 threads and across 1, this is tied down by a slanting stitch over the centre thread. Each row encroaches on the previous one.

Stem stitch (*Fig. 16*)

A back stitch is worked between the completed rows of this stitch. This can be in a darker tone of the same colour or in a different colour or texture; many different effects are possible with this stitch.

Eyelets (*Fig. 17*)

This can be worked over a square of 4 or more threads (*Fig. 17a*)

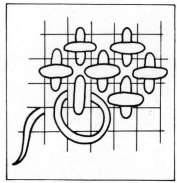

Fig. 11. Upright cross stitch

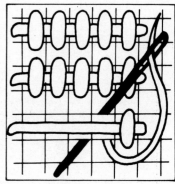

Fig. 12. Upright Gobelin

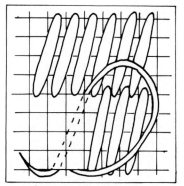

Fig. 13. Encroaching Gobelin

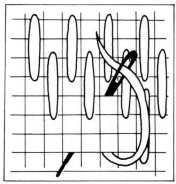

Fig. 14. Bricking

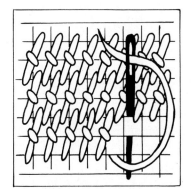

Fig. 15. Knotted stitch

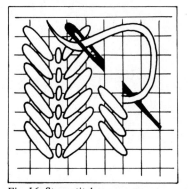

Fig. 16. Stem stitch

Fig. 17. Eyelets. *(a)* square; *(b)* diamond

or over a diamond (*Fig. 17b*). A slight pull is exerted on the yarn to make it lie smoothly at the centre. This stitch usually needs a finer wool than most other stitches on the same mesh. The eyelets need not be symmetrical, one diagram shows.

Usually the canvas shows between the stitches; it can be covered by a back stitch, as in the diagram of diamond eyelets. You can use back stitches with other stitches, but always be sure that it improves the appearance.

Red/green belt. Worked in three strands of crewel wool on double 10s canvas, splitting the ground vertically only *(by Joan Fuller)*.

Canvas work buckle. Worked in wool on single 14s canvas, mounted on thick card and backed with fabric *(by Wendy Meyer)*.

Pink/blue belt. Worked in crepe double knitting on double 12s canvas *(by Anne West)*.

Blue/green/grey belt. Worked in 16s canvas in knitting and crewel wools. The background is in tent stitch, with a raised pattern in multiple cross, mosaic, crossed corner and back stitch *(by Georgette Johnson)*.

Bag with suede mount. Worked on 10s canvas in two-ply rug wool, tapestry wool and coton perle in Florentine stitch (Bargello) *(by Nora Jones)*.

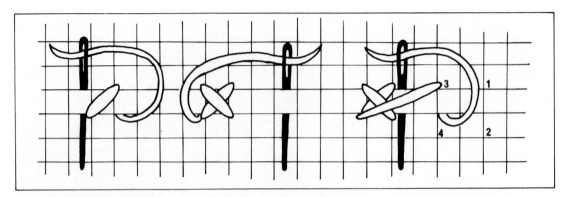

Fig. 18. Long-armed cross

Long-armed cross (*Fig. 18*)

Begin and end with a cross stitch. After this, go forward 4 threads and back 2. The work can be turned and the stitch worked back under the first row, giving a good plaited effect. You can also work in blocks, alternately vertical and horizontal.

Free stitches (*Figs. 19 and 20*)

There is no need to stick to the rules all the time. Vary the number of threads to suit your work. Build up areas with stitches of different sizes. Try some of the stitches you know from other forms of embroidery.

DESIGNING

Ideas for design come from many different sources: a photograph you have seen, a drawing, an illustration in a magazine or book, an arrangement of cut paper shapes.

You can draw designs on graph paper and count them on to the canvas. Remember that a curved line becomes stepped in canvas work and this stepping is more pronounced on large

Fig. 19. Free eyelets

Fig. 20. Free Gobelin

mesh canvases and in large stitches (*Fig. 21*). Do not aim at very small shapes or intricate curves on the coarser canvases.

Tack simple designs on the canvas. Cut paper shapes may be pinned on to the canvas and a tacking line put round them.

If you prefer a more definite line, go over the drawing with ink. Put the paper under the canvas, check that any horizontal or vertical lines on the drawing tally with the threads of the canvas, and secure with weights or drawing pins (thumb tacks). Now go over the lines on the canvas with a brush and waterproof ink (*Fig. 22*). Make sure that the ink really is waterproof or it will run into the wools when the work is stretched.

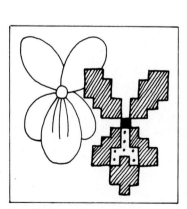

Fig. 21. Curved lines become stepped on canvas

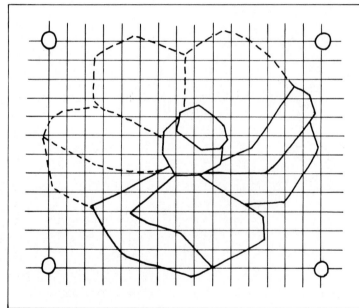

Fig. 22. Transferring a design in ink

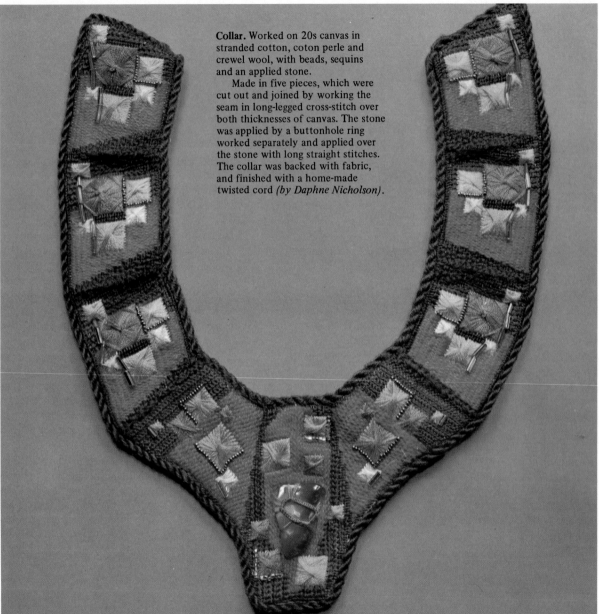

Collar. Worked on 20s canvas in stranded cotton, coton perle and crewel wool, with beads, sequins and an applied stone.

Made in five pieces, which were cut out and joined by working the seam in long-legged cross-stitch over both thicknesses of canvas. The stone was applied by a buttonhole ring worked separately and applied over the stone with long straight stitches. The collar was backed with fabric, and finished with a home-made twisted cord *(by Daphne Nicholson)*.

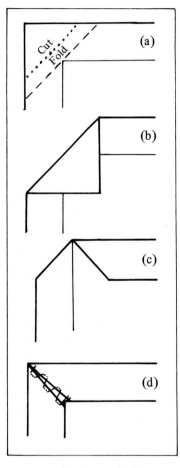

Fig. 23. Mitring. *(a)* The fold (dashes) is made on the corner of the finished work. If you need to cut, cut on the dotted line; *(b)* turn over on the fold line; *(c)* turn over the top edge; *(d)* turn over the other edge and slip stitch

The background

Look at the background shapes before beginning. Put tracing paper over the design and block them in (felt tip markers do this very quickly). You can now see which of these shapes are pleasing and alter any which are not.

Choose stitches to make a foil to the rest of the work: small, smooth stitches against big chunky ones, patterned stitches against plain. Some smaller stitches, like tent, take a long time to work, so, if time is limited, you may like to work big stitches at random, surrounded by tent stitches. Or, if it fits the design, you may prefer to vary the colour by working with two strands of pale crewel wool and one strand of a medium tone, then one strand pale and two strands medium.

You can also mix stitches; the character of the design may suggest how this is to be done. If the design source is a photograph, you may find a texture which suggests the stitches to use. Wind blowing the leaves of the poppies suggested the treatment of the background for the 'Poppies' panel shown on page 3. The mixture of stitches and colour helped the work along.

STRETCHING

Do not iron the canvas. If you do, the size with which it has been stiffened will melt into the wools. If you work in a frame, tighten the pegs and strings, check that the edges are at right angles and damp the work on both sides. Leave it to dry at room temperature for at least 24 hours.

If your piece has been worked in the hand, you will need a flat board, three sheets of white blotting paper larger than the work, or an equivalent thickness of white cotton fabric, rustless drawing pins (thumbtacks) and a set square. Put the blotting paper or cotton on the board and damp the back of the work. Then put

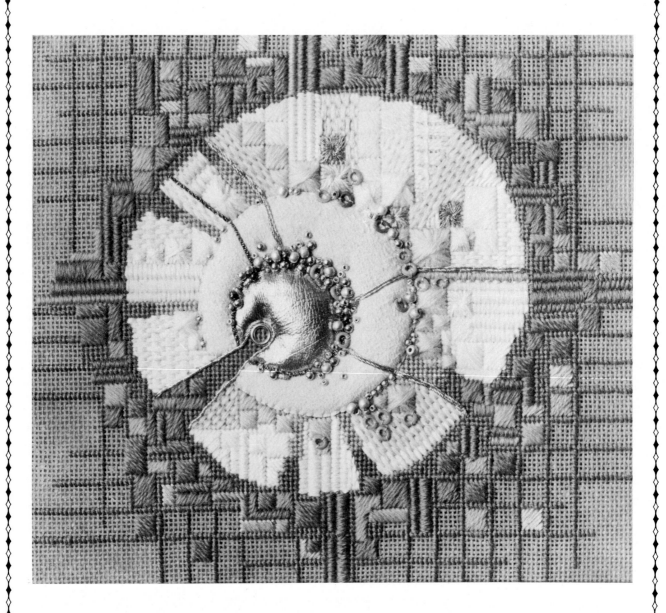

Panel: 'Seedhead'. Canvas embroidery, leaving some of the background unworked. The design was based on a dried seedhead, and was embroidered in knitting wools, stranded cottons, padded chamois leather, gold kid, metal threads and beads *(by Jan Messent)*.

the work face up on the blotting paper and pin along the top edge, keeping it straight and taut. Now pin the opposite edge and then the third and fourth sides, using the set square to check that the sides are at right angles, gently pulling so that the work is under slight tension. Leave it to dry as with the framed work. Sometimes badly distorted work needs more than one stretching.

MAKING UP

Mitring (*Fig. 23*)

Mitring makes a neat corner. Follow the steps shown in *Fig. 23* and cut the corner only if really necessary to avoid bulk; oversew it immediately.

Edging (*Fig. 24*)

This stitch can be used for finishing edges of belts, the tops of purses and spectacle cases and for joining backs and fronts of cushions, purses or pencil cases. Leave two threads unworked until making up for edging. If you are attaching a fabric back to a canvas work front, use a chenille needle. The stitch is worked just like long armed cross but there is an extra stitch which gives a good cover to the edge.

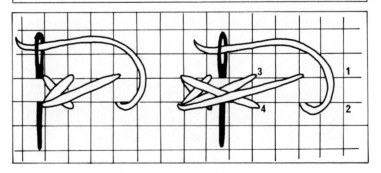

Fig. 24. Edge stitch

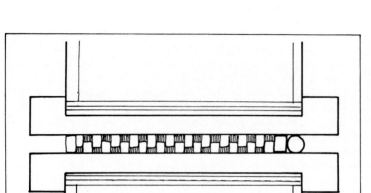

Doorstop. A brick covered with canvas work, with felt on the base. The design was based on a knot in a plank of wood. The applied pieces were padded with felt and sewn on before the canvas was worked *(by Lois Hennequin)*.

Fig. 25. Inserting a zip in a purse

Zips (*Fig. 25*)

Back stitch zips between the edging stitch and the rest of the work.

Interlining

Make the interlining a fraction smaller than the finished canvas. Pin and tack the work over the interlining. Allow for the curve on a belt, keeping the canvas on a curve as you put in the interlining. Catch down with herringbone or catch stitching and avoid too tight a pull on the stitches (*Fig. 26*)

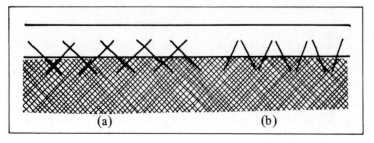

(a)   (b)

Fig. 26. Catching down on to an interlining. *(a)* Herringbone; *(b)* catch stitch

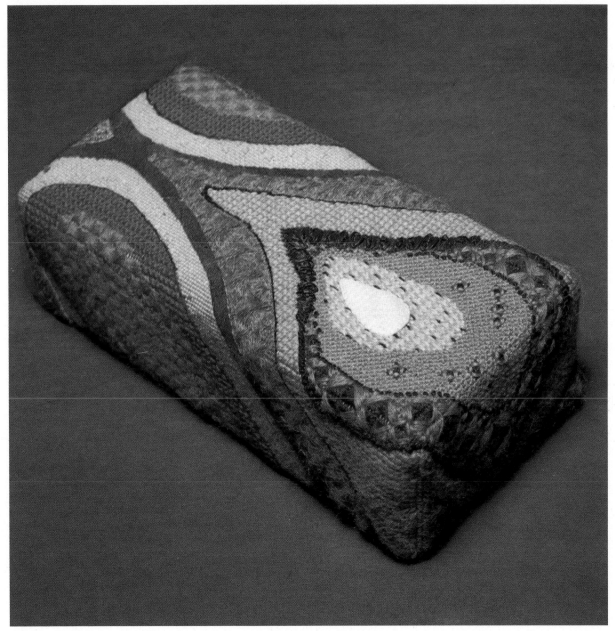

Grey/black bag. Worked on single 14s canvas, using four-ply knitting yarns. The design is worked in straight stitch with the background in tent stitch. The bag has a fabric gusset and strap, and is stiffened with buckram *(by Wendy Meyer)*.

Panel: 'Landscape'. Worked on 22s canvas in crewel wool and stranded cotton, using straight stitches and tent stitches, and leaving much of the canvas unworked *(by Nora Jones)*.

Panels

Cut mounting card a fraction smaller than the finished panel and centre it on the wrong side of the work. Lace from the centres outwards with a strong thread (*Fig. 27*). Use adhesives if you wish.

Fig. 27. Lacing a panel

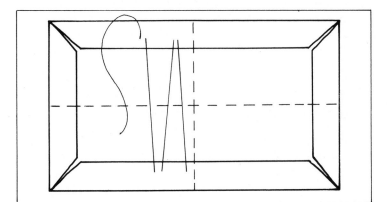

Edited by Kit Pyman
Text and drawings by Nora Jones
Photographs by Search Press Studios

Text, illustrations, arrangement and typography
copyright © Search Press Limited 1978

First published in Great Britain in 1978 by Search
Press Limited, Wellwood, North Farm Road,
Tunbridge Wells, Kent TN2 3DR

Reprinted 1982, 1984, 1986, 1988, 1989

ISBN 0 85532 409 0

Made and printed in Spain by A. G. Elkar, S. Coop.
Autonomía, 71 - 48012-Bilbao - Spain

Inside front cover:
Lamp bases. Worked on 20s canvas
in crewel wools, stranded cotton and
metal threads, with applied gold
kid, beads and stones.

   The canvas was fitted over card-
board rolls. Half-inch turning should
be allowed for the vertical edge, but
allow more as canvas 'takes up' in
working. The top and base are
available from craft shops (fittings
used in basket making). The small
gaps top and bottom are covered
with toning braid. The stands are
weighted with a plastic bag of sand
placed inside *(by Charm Chandler)*.

Back cover:
Panel: 'Beetle'. Worked on 18s
canvas in tapestry wools. The beetle
is mostly in embroidery stitches, the
background in cross stich and
Hungarian stitch *(by Kit Pyman)*.

Front cover:
Florentine work cushion. Worked
on double 12s canvas in double
knitting yarns *(by Anne West)*.